Who Moved My Cheese?

for
Teens

A Note From The Author

Many people all around the world who have read the original edition of *Who Moved My Cheese?* say they wish they had known "The Cheese Story" when they were younger. They realize it would have made everything easier for them.

As a teen, you are likely to face many more changes during your lifetime than your parents or grandparents did. Wouldn't it be great if *you* knew how to deal with change early in your life—and win!

In the story that follows, you can discover how to see changes coming before most people do; how not to take yourself too seriously; and how to adapt quickly—to *Move with the Cheese!*—so that you can make any change work to your advantage.

Whatever changing situation you find yourself in, I hope you use what you uncover in the story to find your own "New Cheese"—whatever is important to you—and that you enjoy it!

The "Who Moved My Cheese?"
Phenomena!

The Story of "Who Moved My Cheese?" was created by Dr. Spencer Johnson to help him deal with a difficult change in his life. It showed him how to take his changing situation seriously but not take himself so seriously.

When his friends noticed how much better life had become for him, and asked why, he revealed his "Cheese" story. Several said, sometimes years later, how hearing the story helped them to keep their sense of humor, to change, and to gain something better themselves. His co-author of *The One Minute Manager*, Ken Blanchard, encouraged him to finally write it as a book to share with many others.

Two decades after the story was created, this book, *Who Moved My Cheese?*, was published. It soon became an accelerating, word-of-mouth #1 International Bestseller, with one million hardcover copies in print within the first sixteen months and over ten million copies in the next two years.

People have reported that what they discovered

in the story has improved their careers, businesses, health and marriages. The "Cheese Story" has found its way into homes, companies, schools, churches, the military, and sports teams. It has spread around the world in many foreign languages. Its appeal is universal.

Critics, on the other hand, do not understand how so many people could find it so valuable. They say the story is so simple a child could understand it, and it insults their intelligence, as it is just obvious common sense. They get nothing out of the story. Some even fear it suggests all change is good and that people should mindlessly conform to unnecessary changes imposed by others, although that is not in the story.

The author has commented that both the fans and critics are "right" in their own way. It is not what is in the story of "Who Moved My Cheese?" but how you interpret it and apply it to your own situation that gives it value.

Hopefully the way you interpret the story of "Who Moved My Cheese?," in this special edition for teens, and put it into action in your life will help you find and enjoy the "New Cheese" you deserve.

Who Moved My Cheese?

for Teens

**An A-Mazing
Way to Change
and Win!**

SPENCER JOHNSON, M.D.

G. P. Putnam's Sons New York

Dedicated to our sons—
Emerson, Christian and Austin

G. P. Putnam's Sons,
a division of Penguin Putnam Books for Young Readers,
345 Hudson Street, New York, NY 10014.
G. P. Putnam's Sons, Reg. U.S. Pat. & Tm. Off.
Published simultaneously in Canada.
Printed in the United States of America.
Jacket art and design by Gina DiMassi.
Library of Congress Cataloging-in-Publication Data
Johnson, Spencer. Who moved my cheese? for teens :
an a-mazing way to change and win / Spencer Johnson.
p. cm. Summary: Presents the author's parable about change
framed in a story about a group of high school friends
trying to handle change in their lives.
1. Change (Psychology)—Juvenile literature.
2. Teenagers—Conduct of life—Juvenile literature.
[1. Change (Psychology) 2. Conduct of life.] I. Title.
BF637.C4 J643 2002   155.2'4—dc21   2002026981
ISBN 0-399-24007-1
10

The best laid schemes
o' mice and men
often go astray.

Robert Burns
1759–1796

Life is no straight and easy corridor along
which we travel free and unhampered,
but a maze of passages,
through which we must seek our way,
lost and confused, now and again
checked in a blind alley.

But always, if we have faith,
a door will open for us,
not perhaps one that we ourselves
would ever have thought of,
but one that will ultimately
prove good for us.

A. J. Cronin

Who Moved My Cheese? for Teens

Contents

Parts of All of Us

The four imaginary characters depicted in this
story—the mice: "Sniff" and "Scurry," and
the Littlepeople: "Hem" and "Haw"—
are intended to represent the simple and
the complex parts of ourselves, regardless of
our age, gender, race or nationality.

Sometimes we may act like

Sniff
Who sniffs out
change early,

or

Scurry
Who scurries
into action,

or

Hem
Who denies and resists
change as he fears it will
lead to something worse,

or

Haw
Who learns to adapt in time
when he sees changing can
lead to something *better!*

Whatever parts of us we choose to use,
we all share something in common:
a need to find our way in the Maze
and succeed in changing times.

A Gathering

A Gathering
City High School
Lunchtime

The bell rang and seven friends ran from their different classes to the cafeteria, meeting at the table where they always had lunch together. They had all just heard the news about the big change at their school, and they wanted to talk about it.

Chris and Melanie got there first. "What do you think?" Chris asked. Melanie just rolled her eyes.

Peter, Kerry, Ana, Carl and Josh arrived moments later with the same question. The principal had just announced a major change in the school's schedule. They would now be on a three-semester program, due to overcrowding.

"I think the change is lousy," Ana exclaimed, tossing her backpack on the floor. "I liked the schedule the way it was. Why do things have to change now?"

"Yeah, this is crazy," Peter agreed. "Now some of us will have to switch teachers."

Chris asked, "So what?"

Josh grumbled, "Just when you get to know how things work, they change the rules! Typical."

"Come on, guys," Chris interjected. "Who knows, maybe things will turn out better. The school is supercrowded, this could help."

"I don't care," said Carl, who had failed three classes last year and was repeating. "I don't want to change."

Kerry started laughing. "So you'd be against it, even if it made things better?"

Carl didn't laugh. "Nothing ever gets better at this school," he said firmly.

Melanie looked across the table. "How can you be so sure? We haven't even tried it out yet."

"I've had enough changes in my life already," Josh interrupted. "And I don't want any more."

Everyone at the table knew what Josh meant. His dad had left when he was a little kid and he'd never gotten over it. He was quietly angry about all the changes that happened in his life after that.

"This is just what I needed," Carl said, sinking down in his seat. "With my luck, I'll be stuck going to school in the new summer semester."

Chris laughed and shook his head.

"You think this is funny?" Josh asked him, scowling.

Chris answered, "I'm not laughing at you. I'm laughing at me. Listening to you guys makes me think about how much I used to be like you."

"Oh, and now you're not?" Josh fired back.

Kerry looked at Chris suspiciously. "You're the only one here who doesn't seem bummed about the new schedule. Do you know something we don't?"

"Yeah," Melanie said, eyeing her friend. "What's up? You're all Mr. Happy Guy lately. Are you in love or something?"

"It's not that," Chris said. "I guess things have changed for me since my uncle told me this story he came across at work. It made me laugh at myself and look at stuff differently than I used to."

"So, what's the story?" Melanie asked.

"It's called *Who Moved My Cheese?*"

The group laughed.

Kerry said, "Strange title. I think I'm going to like it. What's it about?"

"It's about these four characters who run through a maze looking for Cheese. The Cheese stands for whatever's important to you—like getting on a team, having a boyfriend or girlfriend, getting into college or just getting out of school and finding a job so you can be free and independent—whatever. The maze is wherever you look for it—like at school."

"Sounds cheesy," Josh joked. They all laughed.

Carl glanced at the clock. "Do we have time for this?" he asked.

"I want to hear it," said Melanie.

"Okay. I'll try to tell it to you just the way my uncle told it to me. The story only takes a little while," Chris told them. "If I start telling it now, I'll be done by the end of lunch."

"Okay," Josh said. "You talk, we'll eat. But this better be good," he added, biting into his sandwich.

"The story is only as good as you want it to be," Chris said. "It all depends on what you want to get from it."

He added, "As you get into the story, you can ask yourself: What is your Cheese and who are you in the story?"

Then he began. . . .

The Story of
Who Moved My Cheese?

The Story

ONCE, long ago in a land far away, there lived four little characters who ran through a Maze looking for cheese to nourish them and make them happy.

Two were mice named "Sniff" and "Scurry" and two were Littlepeople—beings who were as small as mice but who looked and acted a lot like people today. Their names were "Hem" and "Haw."

Due to their small size, it would be easy not to notice what the four of them were doing. But if you looked closely enough, you could discover the most amazing things!

Every day the mice and the Littlepeople spent time in the Maze looking for their own special cheese.

The mice, Sniff and Scurry, possessing simple brains and good instincts, searched for the hard nibbling cheese they liked, as mice often do.

The two Littlepeople, Hem and Haw, used their complex brains, filled with many beliefs and emotions, to search for a very different kind of Cheese—with a capital C—which they believed would make them feel happy and successful.

As different as the mice and Littlepeople were, they shared something in common: every morning, they each put on their jogging suits and running shoes, left their little homes, and raced out into the Maze looking for their favorite cheese.

The Maze was a labyrinth of corridors and chambers, some containing delicious cheese. But there were also dark corners and blind alleys leading nowhere. It was an easy place for anyone to get lost.

However, for those who found their way, the Maze held secrets that let them enjoy a better life.

The mice, Sniff and Scurry, used the simple trial-and-error method of finding cheese. They ran down one corridor, and if it proved empty, they turned and ran down another. They remembered the corridors that held no cheese and quickly went into new areas.

Sniff would smell out the general direction of the cheese, using his great nose, and Scurry would race ahead. They got lost, as you might expect, went off in the wrong direction and often bumped into walls. But after a while, they found their way.

Like the mice, the two Littlepeople, Hem and Haw, also used their ability to think and learn from their past experiences. However, they relied on their complex brains to develop more sophisticated methods of finding Cheese.

Sometimes they did well, but at other times their powerful human beliefs and emotions took over and clouded the way they looked at things. It made life in the Maze more complicated and challenging.

Nonetheless, Sniff, Scurry, Hem and Haw all discovered, in their own way, what they were looking for. They each found their own kind of cheese one day at the end of one of the corridors in Cheese Station C.

Every morning after that, the mice and the Littlepeople dressed in their running gear and headed over to Cheese Station C. It wasn't long before they each established their own routine.

Sniff and Scurry continued to wake early every day and race through the Maze, always following the same route.

When they arrived at their destination, the mice took off their running shoes, tied them together and hung them around their necks—so they could get to them quickly whenever they needed them again. Then they enjoyed the cheese.

In the beginning Hem and Haw also raced toward Cheese Station C every morning to enjoy the tasty new morsels that awaited them.

But after a while, a different routine set in for the Littlepeople.

Hem and Haw awoke each day a little later, dressed a little slower, and walked to Cheese Station C. After all, they knew where the Cheese was now and how to get there.

They had no idea where the Cheese came from, or who put it there. They just assumed it would be there.

As soon as Hem and Haw arrived at Cheese Station C each morning, they settled in and made themselves at home. They hung up their jogging suits, put away their running shoes and put on their slippers. They were becoming very comfortable now that they had found the Cheese.

"This is great," Hem said. "There's enough Cheese here to last us forever." The Littlepeople felt happy and successful, and thought they were now secure.

It wasn't long before Hem and Haw regarded the Cheese they found at Cheese Station C as their cheese. It was such a large store of Cheese that they eventually moved their homes to be closer to it, and built a social life around it.

To make themselves feel more at home, Hem and Haw decorated the walls with sayings. One read:

Having Cheese
Makes You
Happy.

Sometimes Hem and Haw would take their friends by to see their pile of Cheese at Cheese Station C, and point to it with pride, saying, "Pretty nice Cheese, huh?" Sometimes they shared it with their friends and sometimes they didn't.

"We deserve this Cheese," Hem said. "We certainly had to work long and hard enough to find it." He picked up a nice fresh piece and ate it.

Afterwards, Hem fell asleep, as he often did.

Every night the Littlepeople would waddle home, full of Cheese, and every morning they would confidently return for more.

This went on for quite some time.

After a while Hem's and Haw's confidence grew into the arrogance of success. Soon they became so comfortable they didn't even notice what was happening.

 As time went on, Sniff and Scurry continued their routine. They arrived early each morning and sniffed and scratched and scurried around Cheese Station C, inspecting the area to see if there had been any changes from the day before. Then they would sit down to nibble on the cheese.

One morning they arrived at Cheese Station C and discovered there was no cheese.

They weren't surprised. Since Sniff and Scurry had noticed the supply of cheese had been getting smaller every day, they were prepared for the inevitable and knew instinctively what to do.

They looked at each other, removed the running shoes they had tied together and hung conveniently around their necks, put them on their feet and laced them up.

The mice did not overanalyze things.

To the mice, the problem and the answer were both simple. The situation at Cheese Station C had changed. So, Sniff and Scurry decided to change.

They both looked out into the Maze. Then Sniff lifted his nose, sniffed, and nodded to Scurry, who took off running through the Maze, while Sniff followed as fast as he could.

They were quickly off in search of New Cheese.

Later that same day, Hem and Haw arrived at Cheese Station C. They had not been paying attention to the small changes that had been taking place each day, so they took it for granted their Cheese would be there.

They were unprepared for what they found.

"What! No Cheese?" Hem yelled. He continued yelling, "No Cheese? No Cheese?" as though if he shouted loud enough, someone would put it back.

"Who moved my Cheese?" he hollered.

Finally, he put his hands on his hips, his face turned red, and he screamed at the top of his voice, "It's not fair!"

Haw just shook his head in disbelief. He, too, had counted on finding Cheese at Cheese Station C. He stood there for a long time, frozen with shock. He was just not ready for this.

Hem was yelling something, but Haw didn't want to hear it. He didn't want to deal with what was facing him, so he just tuned everything out.

The Littlepeoples' behavior was not very attractive or productive, but it was understandable.

Finding Cheese wasn't easy, and it meant a great deal more to the Littlepeople than just having enough of it to eat every day.

Finding Cheese was the Littlepeoples' way of getting what they thought they needed to be happy. They had their own ideas of what Cheese meant to them, depending on their taste.

For some, finding Cheese was having material things, or becoming a great athlete or famous star. For others it was doing well in school, having a wonderful relationship or feeling good about themselves.

For Haw, Cheese just meant feeling safe, having a loving family someday and living in a cozy cottage on Cheddar Lane.

To Hem, Cheese was becoming a Big Cheese in charge of others and owning a big house atop Camembert Hill.

Because Cheese was important to them, the two Littlepeople spent a long time trying to decide what to do. All they could think of was to keep looking around Cheeseless Station C to see if the Cheese was really gone.

While Sniff and Scurry had quickly moved on, Hem and Haw continued to hem and haw.

They ranted and raved at the injustice of it all. Haw started to get depressed. What would happen if the Cheese wasn't there tomorrow? He had made future plans based on this Cheese.

The Littlepeople couldn't believe it. How could this have happened? No one had warned them. It wasn't right. It was not the way things were supposed to be.

Hem and Haw went home that night hungry and discouraged. But before they left, Haw wrote on the wall:

The More Important
Your Cheese Is To You
The More You Want
To Hold On To It.

The next day Hem and Haw left their homes and returned to Cheese Station C again, where they still expected, somehow, to find their Cheese.

The situation hadn't changed, the Cheese was no longer there. The Littlepeople didn't know what to do. Hem and Haw just stood there, immobilized like two statues.

Haw shut his eyes as tight as he could and put his hands over his ears. He just wanted to block everything out. He didn't want to know the Cheese supply had gradually been getting smaller. He believed it had been moved all of a sudden.

Hem analyzed the situation over and over and eventually his complicated brain with its huge belief system took hold. "Why did they do this to me?" he demanded. "What's really going on here?"

Finally, Haw opened his eyes, looked around and said, "By the way, where are Sniff and Scurry? Do you think they know something we don't?"

Hem scoffed, "What would they know?"

Hem continued, "They're just mice. They just respond to what happens. We're Littlepeople. We're smarter than mice. We should be able to figure this out."

"I know we're smarter," Haw said, "but we don't seem to be acting smarter at the moment. Things are changing around here, Hem. Maybe we need to change and do things differently."

"Why should we change?" Hem asked. "We're Littlepeople. We're special. This sort of thing should not happen to us. Or if it does, we should at least get some benefits."

"Why should we get benefits?" Haw asked.

"Because we're entitled," Hem claimed.

"Entitled to what?" Haw wanted to know.

"We're entitled to our Cheese."

"Why?" Haw asked.

"Because, we didn't cause this problem," Hem said. "Somebody else did this and we should get something out of it."

Haw suggested, "Maybe we should simply stop analyzing the situation so much and go find some New Cheese?"

"Oh no," Hem argued. "I'm going to get to the bottom of this."

While Hem and Haw were still trying to decide what to do, Sniff and Scurry were already well on their way. They went farther into the Maze, up and down corridors, looking for cheese in every Cheese Station they could find.

They didn't think of anything else but finding New Cheese.

They didn't find any for some time until they finally went into an area of the Maze where they had never been before: Cheese Station N.

They squealed with delight. They found what they had been looking for: a great supply of New Cheese.

They could hardly believe their eyes. It was the biggest store of cheese the mice had ever seen.

In the meantime, Hem and Haw were still back in Cheese Station C evaluating their situation. They were now suffering from the effects of having no Cheese. They were becoming frustrated and angry and were blaming each other for the situation they were in.

Now and then Haw thought about his mice friends, Sniff and Scurry, and wondered if they had found any cheese yet. He believed they might be having a hard time, as running through the Maze usually involved some uncertainty. But he also knew that it was likely to only last for a while.

Sometimes, Haw would imagine Sniff and Scurry finding New Cheese and enjoying it. He thought about how good it would be for him to be out on an adventure in the Maze, and to find fresh New Cheese. He could almost taste it.

The more clearly Haw saw the image of himself finding and enjoying the New Cheese, the more he saw himself leaving Cheese Station C.

"Let's go!" he exclaimed, all of a sudden.

"No," Hem quickly responded. "I like it here. It's comfortable. It's what I know. Besides, it's dangerous out there."

"No it isn't," Haw argued. "We've run through many parts of the Maze before, and we can do it again."

"I'm getting too old for that," Hem said. "And I'm afraid I'm not interested in getting lost and making a fool of myself. Are you?"

With that, Haw's fear of failing returned and his hope of finding New Cheese faded.

So every day, the Littlepeople continued to do what they had done before. They went to Cheese Station C, found no Cheese, and returned home, carrying their worries and frustrations with them.

They tried to deny what was happening, but found it harder to get to sleep, had less energy the next day, and were becoming irritable.

Their homes were not the nurturing places they once were. The Littlepeople had difficulty sleeping and were having nightmares about not finding any Cheese.

But Hem and Haw still returned to Cheese Station C and waited there every day.

Hem said, "You know, if we just work harder, we'll find that nothing has really changed that much. The Cheese is probably nearby. Maybe they just hid it behind the wall."

The next day, Hem and Haw returned with tools. Hem held the chisel while Haw banged on the hammer until they made a hole in the wall of Cheese Station C. They peered inside but found no Cheese.

They were disappointed but believed they could solve the problem. So they started earlier, stayed longer, and worked harder. But after a while, all they had was a large hole in the wall.

Haw was beginning to realize the difference between activity and productivity.

"Maybe," Hem said, "we should just sit here and see what happens. Sooner or later they have to put the Cheese back."

Haw wanted to believe that. So each day he went home to rest and returned reluctantly with Hem to Cheese Station C. But Cheese never reappeared.

By now the Littlepeople were growing weak from hunger and stress. Haw was getting tired of just waiting for their situation to improve. He began to see that the longer they stayed in their Cheeseless situation, the worse off they would be.

Haw knew they were losing their edge.

Finally, one day Haw began laughing at himself. "Haw, haw, look at us. We keep doing the same things over and over again and wonder why things don't get better. If this wasn't so ridiculous, it would be even funnier."

Haw did not like the idea of having to run through the Maze again, because he knew he would get lost and have no idea where he would find any Cheese. But he had to laugh at his folly when he saw what his fear was doing to him.

He asked Hem, "Where did we put our running shoes?" It took a long time to find them because they had put everything away when they found their Cheese at Cheese Station C, thinking they wouldn't be needing them anymore.

As Hem saw his friend getting into his running gear, he said, "You're not really going out into the Maze again, are you? Why don't you just wait here with me until they put the Cheese back?"

"Because, you just don't get it," Haw said. "I didn't want to see it either, but now I realize they're never going to put yesterday's Cheese back. It's time to find New Cheese."

Hem argued, "But what if there is no Cheese out there? Or even if there is, what if you don't find it?"

"I don't know," Haw said. He had asked himself those same questions too many times and felt the fears again that kept him where he was.

He asked himself, "Where am I more likely to find Cheese—here or in the Maze?"

He painted a picture in his mind. He saw himself venturing out into the Maze with a smile on his face.

While this picture surprised him, it made him feel good. He saw himself getting lost now and then in the Maze, but felt confident he would eventually find New Cheese out there and all the good things that came with it. He gathered his courage.

Then he used his imagination to paint the most believable picture he could—with the most realistic details—of him finding and enjoying the taste of New Cheese.

He saw himself eating Swiss cheese with holes in it, bright orange Cheddar and American cheeses, Italian Mozzarella and wonderfully soft French Camembert cheese, and . . .

Then he heard Hem say something and realized they were still at Cheese Station C.

Haw said, "Sometimes, Hem, things change and they are never the same again. This looks like one of those times. That's life! Life moves on. And so should we."

Haw looked at his emaciated companion and tried to talk sense to him, but Hem's fear had turned into anger and he wouldn't listen.

Haw didn't mean to be rude to his friend, but he had to laugh at how silly they both looked.

As Haw prepared to leave, he started to feel more alive, knowing that he was finally able to laugh at himself, let go and move on.

Haw laughed and announced, "It's . . . Maze . . . time!"

Hem didn't laugh and he didn't respond.

Haw picked up a small, sharp rock and wrote a serious thought on the wall for Hem to think about, hoping it would help Hem to go after the New Cheese. Hem didn't want to see it.

It read:

If You Do Not
Change,
You Can Become
Extinct.

Then, Haw stuck his head out and peered anxiously into the Maze. He thought about how he'd gotten himself into this Cheeseless situation.

He had believed that there may not be any Cheese in the Maze, or he may not find it. Such fearful beliefs were immobilizing and killing him.

Haw smiled. He knew Hem was wondering, "Who moved my cheese?" but Haw was wondering, "Why didn't I get up and move with the Cheese sooner?"

As he started out into the Maze, Haw looked back to where he had come from and felt its comfort. He could feel himself being drawn back into familiar territory—even though he hadn't found Cheese here for some time.

Haw became more anxious and wondered if he really wanted to go out into the Maze. He wrote a saying on the wall ahead of him and stared at it for some time:

What Would You Do
If You Weren't Afraid?

He thought about it.

He knew sometimes some fear can be good. When you are afraid things are going to get worse if you don't do something, it can prompt you into action. But it is not good when you are so afraid that it keeps you from doing anything.

He looked to his right, to the part of the Maze where he had never been, and felt the fear.

Then, he took a deep breath, turned right into the Maze, and jogged slowly, into the unknown.

As he tried to find his way, Haw worried, at first, that he might have waited too long in Cheese Station C. He hadn't had any Cheese for so long that he was now weak. It took him longer and it was more painful than usual to get through the Maze.

He decided that if he ever got the chance again, he would get out of his comfort zone and adapt to change sooner. It would make things easier.

Then, Haw smiled a weak smile as he thought, "Better late than never."

During the next several days, Haw found a little Cheese here and there, but nothing that lasted very long. He had hoped to find enough Cheese to take some back to Hem and encourage him to come out into the Maze.

But Haw didn't feel confident enough yet. He had to admit he found it confusing in the Maze. Things seemed to have changed since the last time he was out here.

Just when he thought he was getting ahead, he would get lost in the corridors. It seemed his progress was two steps forward and one step backwards. It was a challenge, but he had to admit that being back in the Maze, hunting for Cheese, wasn't nearly as bad as he feared it might be.

As time went on he began to wonder if it was realistic for him to expect to find New Cheese. He wondered if he had bitten off more than he could chew. Then he laughed, realizing that he had nothing to chew on at that moment.

Whenever he started to get discouraged, he reminded himself that what he was doing, as uncomfortable as it was at the moment, was in reality much better than staying in the Cheeseless situation. He was taking control, rather than simply letting things happen to him.

Then he reminded himself, if Sniff and Scurry could move on, so could he!

Later, as Haw looked back on things, he realized that the Cheese at Cheese Station C had not just disappeared overnight, as he had once believed. The amount of Cheese that had been there towards the end had been getting smaller, and what was left had grown old. It didn't taste as good.

Mold may even have begun to grow on the Old Cheese, although he hadn't noticed it. He had to admit, however, that if he had wanted to, he probably could have seen what was coming. But he didn't.

Haw now realized that the change probably would not have taken him by surprise if he had been watching what was happening all along and if he had anticipated change. Maybe that's what Sniff and Scurry had been doing.

He decided he would stay more alert from now on. He would expect change to happen and look for it. He would trust his basic instincts to sense when change was going to occur and be ready to adapt to it.

He stopped for a rest and wrote on the wall of the Maze:

Smell The Cheese Often
So You Know
When It Is Getting Old.

Sometime later, after not finding Cheese for what seemed like a long time, Haw finally came across a huge Cheese Station, which looked promising. When he went inside, however, he was most disappointed to discover that the Cheese Station was empty.

"This empty feeling has happened to me too often," he thought. He felt like giving up.

Haw was losing his physical strength. He knew he was lost and was afraid he would not survive. He thought about turning around and heading back to Cheese Station C. At least, if he made it back, and Hem was still there, Haw wouldn't be alone. Then he asked himself the same question again: "What would I do if I weren't afraid?"

Haw thought he was past his fear, but he was afraid more often than he liked to admit, even to himself. He wasn't always sure what he was afraid of, but, in his weakened condition, he knew now he was simply fearful of going on alone. Haw didn't know it, but he was running behind because he was still weighed down by fearful beliefs.

Haw wondered if Hem had moved on, or if he was still paralyzed by his own fears. Then, Haw remembered the times when he had felt his best in the Maze. It was when he was moving along.

He wrote on the wall, knowing it was as much a reminder to himself as it was a marking for his friend Hem, hopefully, to follow:

Movement In A
New Direction
Helps You Find
New Cheese.

Haw looked down the dark passageway and was aware of his fear. What lay ahead? Was it empty? Or worse, were there dangers lurking? He began to imagine all kinds of frightening things that could happen to him. He was scaring himself to death.

Then he laughed at himself. He realized his fears were making things worse. So he did what he would do if he weren't afraid. He moved in a new direction.

As he started running down the dark corridor, he began to smile. Haw didn't realize it yet, but he was discovering what nourished his soul. He was letting go and trusting what lay ahead for him, even though he did not know exactly what it was.

To his surprise, Haw started to enjoy himself more and more. "Why do I feel so good?" he wondered. "I don't have any Cheese and I don't know where I am going."

Before long, he knew why he felt good.

He stopped to write again on the wall:

When You Stop
Being Afraid,
You Feel Good!

Haw realized he had been held captive by his own fear. Moving in a new direction had freed him.

Now he felt the cool breeze that was blowing in this part of the Maze and it was refreshing. He took in some deep breaths and felt invigorated by the movement. Once he had gotten past his fear, it turned out to be more enjoyable than he once believed it could be.

Haw hadn't felt this way for a long time. He had almost forgotten how much fun it was to go for it.

To make things even better, Haw started to paint a picture in his mind again. He saw himself in great realistic detail, sitting in the middle of a pile of all his favorite cheeses—from Cheddar to Brie! He saw himself eating the many cheeses he liked, and he enjoyed what he saw. Then he imagined how much he would enjoy all their great tastes.

The more clearly he saw the image of himself enjoying New Cheese, the more real and believable it became. He could sense that he was going to find it.

He wrote:

Imagining Yourself
Enjoying Your
New Cheese
Leads You To It.

Haw kept thinking about what he could gain instead of what he was losing.

He wondered why he had always thought that a change would lead to something worse. Now he realized that change could lead to something better.

"Why didn't I see this before?" he asked himself.

Then he raced through the Maze with greater strength and agility. Before long he spotted a Cheese Station and became excited as he noticed little pieces of New Cheese near the entrance.

They were types of Cheese he had never seen before, but they looked great. He tried them and found that they were delicious. He ate most of the New Cheese bits that were available and put a few in his pocket to have later and perhaps share with Hem. He began to regain his strength.

He entered the Cheese Station with great excitement. But, to his dismay, he found it was empty. Someone had already been there and had left only the few bits of New Cheese.

He realized that if he had moved sooner, he would very likely have found a good deal of New Cheese here.

Haw decided to go back and see if Hem was ready to join him.

As he retraced his steps, he stopped and wrote on the wall:

The Quicker You Let Go
of Old Cheese,
The Sooner You Find
New Cheese.

After a while Haw made his way back to Cheese Station C and found Hem. He offered Hem bits of New Cheese, but was turned down.

Hem appreciated his friend's gesture but said, "I don't think I would like New Cheese. It's not what I'm used to. I want my own Cheese back and I'm not going to change until I get what I want."

Haw just shook his head in disappointment and reluctantly went back out on his own. As he returned to the farthest point he had reached in the Maze, he missed his friend, but realized he liked what he was discovering. Even before he found what he hoped would be a great supply of New Cheese, if ever, he knew that what made him happy wasn't just having Cheese.

He was happy when he wasn't being run by his fear. He liked what he was doing now.

Knowing this, Haw didn't feel as weak as he did when he stayed in Cheese Station C with no Cheese. Just realizing he was not letting his fear stop him, and knowing that he had taken a new direction, nourished him and gave him strength.

Now he felt that it was just a question of time before he found what he needed. In fact, he sensed he had already found what he was looking for.

He smiled, as he realized:

It Is Safer To
Search In The Maze
Than Remain In A
Cheeseless Situation.

Haw realized again, as he had once before, that what you are afraid of is never as bad as what you imagine. The fear you let build up in your mind is worse than the situation that actually exists.

He'd been so afraid of never finding New Cheese that he didn't even want to start looking. But since starting his journey, he had found enough Cheese in the corridors to keep him going. Now he looked forward to finding more. Just looking ahead was becoming exciting.

His old thinking had been clouded by his worries and fears. He used to think about not having enough Cheese, or not having it last as long as he wanted. He used to think more about what could go wrong than what could go right.

But that had changed in the days since he had left Cheese Station C.

He used to believe that Cheese should never be moved and that change wasn't right.

Now he realized it was natural for change to continually occur, whether you expect it or not. Change could surprise you only if you didn't expect it and weren't looking for it.

When he realized he had changed his beliefs, he paused to write on the wall:

Old Beliefs
Do Not Lead You
To New Cheese.

Haw hadn't found any Cheese yet, but as he ran through the Maze, he thought about what he had already learned.

Haw now realized that his new beliefs were encouraging new behaviors. He was behaving differently than when he kept returning to the same Cheeseless station.

He knew that when you change what you believe, you change what you do.

You can believe that a change will harm you and resist it. Or you can believe that finding New Cheese will help you and embrace the change.

It all depends on what you choose to believe.

He wrote on the wall:

When You See That
You Can Find And
Enjoy New Cheese,
You Change Course.

Haw knew he would be in better shape now if he had dealt with the change much sooner and left Cheese Station C earlier. He would feel stronger in body and spirit and he could have coped better with the challenge of finding New Cheese. In fact, he probably would have found it by now if he had expected change, rather than wasting time denying that the change had already taken place.

He used his imagination again and saw himself finding and savoring New Cheese. He decided to proceed into the more unknown parts of the Maze, and found little bits of Cheese here and there. Haw began to regain his strength and confidence.

As he thought back on where he had come from, Haw was glad he had written on the wall in many places. He trusted that it would serve as a marked trail for Hem to follow through the Maze, if he ever chose to leave Cheese Station C.

Haw just hoped he was heading in the right direction. He thought about the possibility that Hem would read The Handwriting On The Wall and find his way.

He wrote on the wall what he had been thinking about for some time:

Noticing
Small Changes Early
Helps You Adapt To
The Bigger Changes
That Are To Come.

By now, Haw had let go of the past and was adapting to the present.

He continued on through the Maze with greater strength and speed. And before long, it happened.

When it seemed like he had been in the Maze forever, his journey—or at least this part of his journey—ended quickly and happily.

Haw proceeded along a corridor that was new to him, rounded a corner, and found New Cheese at Cheese Station N!

When he went inside, he was startled by what he saw. Piled high everywhere was the greatest supply of Cheese he had ever seen. He didn't recognize all that he saw, as some kinds of Cheese were new to him.

Then he wondered for a moment whether it was real or just his imagination, until he saw his old friends Sniff and Scurry.

Sniff welcomed Haw with a nod of his head, and Scurry waved his paw. Their fat little bellies showed that they had been here for some time.

Haw quickly said his hellos and soon took bites of every one of his favorite Cheeses. He pulled off his shoes, tied the laces together, and hung them around his neck in case he needed them again.

Sniff and Scurry laughed. They nodded their heads in admiration. Then Haw jumped into the New Cheese. When he had eaten his fill, he lifted a piece of fresh Cheese and made a toast. "Hooray for Change!"

As Haw enjoyed the New Cheese, he reflected on what he had learned.

He realized that when he had been afraid to change, he had been holding on to the illusion of Old Cheese that was no longer there.

So what was it that made him change? Was it the fear of starving to death? Haw smiled as he thought it certainly helped.

Then he laughed and realized that he had started to change as soon as he had learned to laugh at himself and at what he had been doing wrong. He realized the fastest way to change is to laugh at your own folly—then you can let go and quickly move on.

He knew he had learned something
useful about moving on from his mice
friends, Sniff and Scurry. They kept
life simple. They didn't overanalyze
or overcomplicate things. When the situation
changed and the Cheese had been moved, they
changed and moved with the Cheese. He would
remember that.

Haw had also used his wonderful brain to do
what Littlepeople do better than mice.

He envisioned himself—in realistic detail—
finding something better—much better.

He reflected on the mistakes he had made in the
past and used them to plan for his future. He knew
that you could learn to deal with change.

You could be more aware of the need to keep
things simple, be flexible, and move quickly.

You did not need to overcomplicate matters or
confuse yourself with fearful beliefs.

You could notice when the little changes began
so that you would be better prepared for the big
change that might be coming.

He knew he needed to adapt faster, for if you do
not adapt in time, you might as well not adapt at all.

He had to admit that the biggest inhibitor to change lies within yourself, and that nothing gets better until you change.

Perhaps most importantly, he realized that there is always New Cheese out there whether you recognize it at the time, or not. And that you are rewarded with it when you go past your fear and enjoy the adventure.

He knew some fear should be respected, as it can keep you out of real danger. But he realized most of his fears were irrational and had kept him from changing when he needed to.

He didn't like it at the time, but he knew that the change had turned out to be a blessing in disguise as it led him to find better Cheese.

He had even found a better part of himself.

As Haw recalled what he had learned, he thought about his friend Hem. He wondered if Hem had read any of the sayings Haw had written on the wall at Cheese Station C and throughout the Maze.

Had Hem ever decided to let go and move on? Had he ever entered the Maze and discovered what could make his life better?

Or was Hem still hemmed in because he would not change?

Haw thought about going back again to Cheese Station C to see if he could find Hem—assuming that Haw could find his way back there. If he found Hem, he thought he might be able to show him how to get out of his predicament. But Haw realized that he had already tried to get his friend to change.

Hem had to find his own way, beyond his comforts and past his fears. No one else could do it for him, or talk him into it. He somehow had to see the advantage of changing himself.

Haw knew he had left a trail for Hem and that he could find his way, if he could just read The Handwriting On The Wall.

He went over and wrote down a summary of what he had learned on the largest wall of Cheese Station N. He smiled as he looked at what he had learned:

THE HANDWRITING ON THE WALL

Change Happens
They Keep Moving The Cheese

Anticipate Change
Get Ready For The Cheese To Move

Monitor Change
Smell The Cheese Often So You
Know When It Is Getting Old

Adapt To Change Quickly
The Quicker You Let Go Of Old Cheese,
The Sooner You Can Enjoy New Cheese

Change
Move With The Cheese

Enjoy Change!
Savor The Adventure And Enjoy
The Taste Of New Cheese!

Be Ready To Change Quickly
And Enjoy It Again & Again
They Keep Moving The Cheese

Haw realized how far he had come since he had been with Hem in Cheese Station C, but knew it would be easy for him to slip back if he got too comfortable. So, each day he inspected Cheese Station N to see what the condition of his Cheese was. He was going to do whatever he could to avoid being surprised by unexpected change.

While Haw still had a great supply of Cheese, he often went out into the Maze and explored new areas to stay in touch with what was happening around him. He knew it was safer to be aware of his real choices than to isolate himself in his comfort zone.

Then, Haw heard what he thought was the sound of movement out in the Maze. As the noise grew louder, he realized that someone was coming.

Could it be that Hem was arriving? Was he about to turn the corner?

Haw said a little prayer and hoped—as he had many times before—that maybe, at last, his friend was finally able to . . .

Move With
The Cheese
And Enjoy It!

The end . . .

or is it
a new beginning?

A Discussion

A Discussion
After Lunch

Chris finished the story just as the bell rang, signaling the end of lunch.

"Wait," Melanie said. "I'm not sure I get this story yet. Can we meet later, maybe at Sharky's?"

"I'm up for it," Josh said as he balled up his napkin and shot it into the trash.

"Cool with me," Kerry chimed in, and everyone else agreed except Carl.

"Not me," Carl told Kerry. "There's a show on tonight I wanna watch."

"You and your TV," Kerry joked. "I'll see the rest of you guys tonight," she said as the group left the cafeteria and went to their afternoon classes.

Later that night, Chris was the first to arrive at Sharky's, the town's pizza parlor. He picked a big, cozy booth in the back, large enough for everybody.

When everyone else got there, they had to decide on toppings for their pizza, always a huge debate. As the group gave their confusing order to the waitress, Ana said, "Can you make sure the cheese on our pizza is new cheese, not old cheese? Thanks." Everyone at the table laughed, and the waitress walked away shaking her head.

"I was thinking about that story all afternoon," Melanie said. "Who do you guys think you're like— Sniff, Scurry, Hem, or Haw?"

"Do we have to pick just one?" Peter asked. "Sometimes I act like Scurry, sometimes I act like Hem, I don't know."

"Yes. I think we're different characters at different times," Ana said, looking to Chris for approval.

"Don't look at me," Chris said. "What you get out of the story is totally up to you."

"I think the cheese can be anything that you want," Kerry said, "or think that you deserve. The maze is where you look for it, like at school or at home."

"Okay," Peter said, "I get it: cheese, maze, mice. But how do you actually use the story? Can anybody give me an example?"

When no one else said anything, Chris offered. "I can. You guys know I played basketball in middle school. I didn't set any records, but I was pretty good. So, when I got to high school, I tried out for the team. I didn't make the cut, and most of the guys who did were taller than me. That made me notice something. It seemed like overnight, my friends, including you, Josh, were getting taller and starting to shave and stuff. I wasn't. I was still wearing the same size jeans I wore in seventh grade.

"Things were changing all around me and I hated what was going on, so I acted like Hem. I kept saying, 'It isn't fair.'" Chris looked at Peter and Josh and admitted, "While you guys were asking girls out and going to dances, I was sitting at home in my room."

"So, what happened?" Melanie asked.

"Well, that's about the same time I heard the Cheese Story. After that, I changed the way I looked at what was going on."

He glanced at Kerry, the tall star of the girls' basketball team, and said, "It was pretty clear that I wasn't going to be drafted by the NBA." Everyone laughed. "So, I decided to be like Haw and laugh about it.

"I stopped taking myself so seriously. It's funny now to think about how much time I wasted worrying about how tall I was—or wasn't. I guess I saw the handwriting on the wall. I couldn't go back to the old cheese station—my seventh-grade dreams of being a basketball star."

"So, what did you do?" Melanie asked again.

"So, I looked for new cheese and I moved on. And now here I am, a starter on the soccer team—something I never knew I was good at. I only wish I'd heard the story sooner."

Peter looked skeptical. "Wait a second. You're saying you got all that from this little story?"

"It's not the story," Chris said. "It's what I took from it. I saw things differently after I heard it. Does that make sense?"

"Your cheese was moved," Melanie started. "But then you heard the story, and saw yourself acting like Hem. So, you lightened up and changed."

Chris nodded and so did a few others. Josh looked deep in thought. "That makes me think about when my dad left," he said, surprising everyone. Josh almost never mentioned his dad. "I wasn't Sniff, because I didn't sniff out what was happening. I never saw it coming."

Josh was quiet for a moment, then he went on. "And I wasn't Scurry, 'cause I didn't know what to do next. I was Hem—and I still am Hem, I guess." Josh took a drink of his soda and looked down. "Waiting for the cheese to come back or something."

Kerry put her arm around her friend's shoulders. "It's not like it's too late to change."

"Yeah," Melanie said, "and being more like Haw doesn't mean you've gotta hit the streets laughing and searching for a new dad."

"Maybe it just means letting go of the old cheese," Ana pointed out. "Like the way your family used to be when your dad was there. Then, going on and finding your new cheese."

Josh asked, "What do you mean—new cheese?"

Melanie, whose parents were also divorced, said, "I think new cheese is just a new way of looking at your situation and acting differently. Like letting go of being mad at your dad for leaving, or always being sad about something you can't change."

"Yeah," Kerry added. "You're not responsible for him leaving, but you are for how you live your life from here on. Maybe it's time to move on and enjoy what you have now."

Ana nudged Josh's leg under the table and said, "Move with the cheese!"

Everyone noticed that Josh smiled. "I guess I've spent so much time thinking about why my dad left—and wishing that he hadn't—that I never thought about, you know, moving on and not letting that one change mess up my whole life."

Chris could see Josh wanted some time to think, so he changed the subject. "Some of the guys on the soccer team know the story. Of course, a few think it's stupid and can't be bothered to get anything out of it.

"But some of our best players say it's helped them let go of stuff that was hurting their game.

"It gives us a secret language to use, too. Like, if someone's holding back in a game, we'll say, 'Don't be such a Hem! Go for it!'"

"I like that!" Kerry said. "We could use that on our girls' team. But you know what really stayed with me from the story was that question, 'What would you do if you weren't afraid of change?'"

Peter claimed, "I'd be on stage by now, with my awesome band." He played a few licks of air guitar.

"If I weren't afraid," Melanie said, "I'd ask Luke out," mentioning the guy she'd had a crush on all year.

Then she turned to Ana and said, "What about you?"

Ana thought about the question for a second. She finally admitted, "I'd probably get in the maze and work on my college applications."

"You haven't yet?" Melanie looked shocked.

Ana shrugged. "No. I haven't wanted to think about graduation 'cause I'm not sure what I want to do. Also, I'm afraid to leave you guys—you're my best friends."

"You're not leaving us. No matter what changes come our way, some basic values, like friendship, will always be the same," Chris said.

"Right," agreed Melanie. "But when things change around us, that's when we have to move with the cheese."

Ana admitted, "I guess I need to change from being a Hem into a Haw before my cheese gets moved at graduation. But I don't know how."

Kerry suggested, "Maybe you should get a picture in your head of new cheese, like Haw did."

"Wasn't that what helped Haw go out into the maze?" Melanie asked the group. "When he imagined himself finding something better—his New Cheese?"

Kerry offered, "Come to think of it, that's what I do just before I shoot a basket. The more clearly I imagine myself making the shot, the more often it goes in."

"So," Ana said, "if I can picture myself next year at college, having a great time, learning new stuff and meeting new friends, then all the changes I have to go through between now and then will seem a lot less scary."

She took a bite of her pizza and tried to see herself on a college campus.

"At least you can admit that you're afraid," Melanie said. "Sometimes I don't think I even know I'm scared of change. I probably hide it under other stuff."

"Like how?" Peter asked.

"Well, like the election last fall," Melanie answered. A groan went up from around the table.

"Do we have to talk about that again?" Peter asked, snagging another slice of pizza.

"Yup," Melanie said. "But this time there's a difference." She pushed up her glasses and went on. "See, I was sure I was going to win class president. Why not? I make the best grades in our class. I didn't even think I'd have to actually do anything to make it happen. I'd done enough already. I found the first cheese station, didn't I? I guess I was pretty arrogant!

"So, why did I lose? Maybe if I'd heard this story sooner, I wouldn't have been boring you guys for months with my excuses and arguments, saying that I lost the election because it's really a popularity contest, and that 'it wasn't fair.'

"Well, now that I look back on it, I was Hem, sitting in that station waiting for my cheese to be put in front of me. When the cheese didn't show up, it was someone else's fault. Come on, guys, tell me, when I was whining about losing, did I sound like Hem?"

"Oh, just a little," Josh said, laughing. Everyone else laughed, too. "But we were right there with you. I guess we're all afraid of change," Josh went on. "It's like any change that you don't decide should happen is automatically a bad thing. Then, when one person says the change is a bad idea, everyone else agrees. Like peer pressure."

"The more I think about who I am in this story," Melanie said, "the more I see the real reason I lost the election. I just decided that being president would look good on my college applications. So, I sat in my comfortable cheese station, waiting, while I should have been out in the maze, sniffing and scurrying. Then I would have found out what kind of class president everybody wanted.

"If I had been more like Haw, I would have been able to see what I was doing wrong, laugh at myself, change what I was doing, and do a lot better. But I didn't . . . so stupid," Melanie said, shaking her head.

"Hey, there's always next year," Kerry said.

Peter laughed, and said, "Haw for President!" making Melanie smile.

Josh finally asked what had been on his mind since lunch. "Do you guys think that Hem ever changed and found his new cheese?"

"I don't know," Kerry said.

"I don't think so," said Ana. "Some people never change and they pay the price for it."

"Just look at us," Melanie told her friends. "Most of us have a story about how we didn't move with the cheese and how it hurt us in the end."

"Oh, come on!" Peter exclaimed, still skeptical. "You guys are taking this way too seriously. There are changes happening every day. I'm sure I've been dealing with them just fine for the past sixteen years of my life without this Cheese Story."

"Maybe the little stuff," Melanie said. "But what about big changes?"

"Look at how we reacted to the change at school today," Kerry interrupted. "None of us sniffed it out. Nobody scurried over to find out what their new schedule was. Instead, we all just sat in our comfortable cheese station, otherwise known as the cafeteria, and complained."

"You're right," Ana said. "And I heard later that the first kids who went to the office to ask about new schedules got to pick what they wanted. They were the Scurrys. Us 'Hems' may be assigned a schedule we don't want."

Chris was glad he was keeping quiet. It was so interesting to see what his friends were getting from the story.

Peter looked around and asked, "Where's Carl?"

"He said he wanted to watch something on TV," Kerry answered. "I could tell he thought the story was stupid from the look on his face, but he's probably the one who needs it the most."

Melanie nodded. "I can see why Carl isn't into this. The story brings up some tough questions, like: What old cheese do I need to let go of? and What new cheese do I need to move on to? Maybe he isn't ready to face that stuff right now."

"Carl reminds me of what I was like when my parents decided to move here," Kerry said. "I didn't want to leave my old friends and I totally resisted the change. It got ugly."

Ana laughed. "I remember that. You refused to talk to anyone here at first."

"Ugh," Kerry groaned in embarrassment, hiding her face in her hands.

"Instead of dealing with the move, I just dug in my heels and acted like a big baby," Kerry admitted. "I blamed my parents for everything and I wouldn't even answer the teacher when she called roll!"

"I didn't know about that," Peter said.

"Me neither," Josh echoed. "Strange. Now we can't get you to stop talking in class."

Kerry kicked Josh under the table. "Anyway," she said, "I wished I'd let go of my old neighborhood and moved on sooner. Would have saved me a lot of hassle."

Ana remarked, "Your cheese got moved, and when you finally dealt with it, you made a whole new group of great friends, if I do say so myself."

"Plus," Peter added, "you've told us you're still friends with the kids in your old town. So, it all turned out pretty good, right?"

"You're totally right," Kerry answered. "But I'm so embarrassed now that I acted that way. I think I owe my parents a 'Sorry about that.'"

Ana put down her piece of pizza and said, "The story made me think of Gavin."

The table went quiet. Gavin was Ana's ex-boyfriend. He had dumped her, hard, after a year of going out. She tried everything to get back with him. It had taken her a long time to get over it.

"I've never admitted, even to myself, that we had problems from the start," Ana began.

"That cheese had some pretty serious mold on it," Josh interrupted, causing everyone to laugh.

"I was so crazy about him," Ana admitted, "and about dating a popular guy, that I decided not to see anything wrong. Gavin was like Sniff, he could see problems ahead. Then, like Haw, he tried to talk to me, but I just acted like Hem. I didn't want to listen. Finally, he left me behind in the old cheese station while he went to Homecoming with his new cheese."

"Sometimes," Peter said, "change just happens. It's like the cheese has a life of its own and it eventually runs out."

"Old cheese isn't your only cheese," Kerry said.

"I guess you're right," Ana sighed.

"Old cheese is like old stuff you do all the time and don't even think about," Melanie pointed out. "Like old behavior that you need to stop."

"You guys are always telling me that I take myself too seriously," Peter said suddenly. "And that I should stop worrying about what everyone else thinks. But if that's my 'old cheese,' I've gotta tell you, it's really hard to stop thinking that way."

"Maybe laughing at your fears would help," Kerry suggested. "It worked for Haw."

"I don't feel like laughing." Peter shook his head. "I want to be taken seriously as a musician. I love playing guitar, but I worry that I'm not good enough. Or that I'll finally get my chance on stage and I'll totally mess up."

Ana asked, "Remember what Melanie said about how Haw painted a picture in his mind, where he saw himself enjoying new cheese? And how that lightened everything up and got him through the maze? Pete, you could paint a picture of your new cheese, too."

"So I should picture myself getting into a band, and playing gigs?" Peter asked.

"That's what you said you'd do if you weren't afraid of change," Chris pointed out.

"You're right," Peter admitted. "I guess my fear of failure has kept me from being a success. That's dumb—like Hem hanging out in that cheese station."

"You should just start your own band," Melanie said. "That's what Haw meant when he wrote *Move With The Cheese* and *Savor The Adventure*. If you're the one making change happen, then you're not so afraid of it."

"I've got an idea," Kerry said. "Can we all think of something better we want—and imagine our new cheese—and talk about it tomorrow at lunch?"

Chris said, "Yeah. And let's see if we can get Carl involved. I know he always acts tough, but he's probably more scared than any of us."

"Cool," Ana said. "I also want to go home and tell my dad and my sisters this story. I'd like to know which characters they think they are, and what our family's new cheese could be."

"I hope it's in the fridge or it's gonna be gross," Josh joked.

Just then, Melanie looked at her watch. "Oh no," she said. "It's getting late, I'm supposed to be home."

Melanie called her mom as the other kids paid the bill. Then she left a good tip for the patient waitress.

Josh stretched his arms over his head. "Time to blow this cheese station," he said, yawning.

"Can you give me a ride through the maze?" Ana asked him jokingly.

"Me, too," Kerry said. "How about you, Pete?" she asked.

"I'm gonna walk," Peter answered. "I've got some stuff to think about."

The friends parted, saying good-bye, anxious to talk more about the story tomorrow and tell it to other friends.

As Josh walked out the door, he stopped and gave Chris a quick bear hug, picking him up from the floor. When Josh put him back down, Chris asked, "What's that for?" since Josh rarely showed affection.

"Thanks for the story, buddy," he said, grinning.

Chris smiled back. "No problem." He had a feeling things were about to change for his friends, at least some of them.

Would Josh be ready to move on and get over the loss of his dad? Would Ana get her college plans in order? Could Peter put aside his self-doubts and perform? How about Melanie and Kerry? Could even Carl change, and get into a good trade school? He was really good at mechanical things. . . .

Then Chris realized that what Carl did was up to Carl.

Who would move with the cheese? Chris wondered. Whoever it was, he knew he was ready to savor the adventure, right along with them.

About the Author

Spencer Johnson, M.D. is one of the most respected and beloved authors in the world. He has inspired and entertained millions with his insightful stories that speak directly to the heart and soul. He has often been referred to as the best there is at taking complex subjects and presenting simple solutions that work.

Dr. Johnson is the author of numerous *New York Times* bestselling books, including the #1 Bestsellers *Who Moved My Cheese?—An A-Mazing Way to Deal with Change at Work and in Life* and *The One Minute Manager®*, the world's most popular management method, written with Kenneth Blanchard.

His education includes a B.A. in psychology from the University of Southern California, an M.D. degree from the Royal College of Surgeons, and medical clerkships at Harvard Medical School and The Mayo Clinic.

Dr. Johnson has served as Medical Director of Communications for Medtronic, the inventors of cardiac pacemakers; Research Physician at the Institute for Inter-Disciplinary Studies, a think tank; Consultant to the Center for the Study of the Person, and to the School of Medicine, University of California; and Leadership Fellow at The Harvard Business School.

His books have been featured often in the media, including CNN, *The Today Show*, *Larry King Live*, *Time*, *Business Week*, *The New York Times*, *Wall Street Journal*, *Fortune*, *USA Today*, Associated Press and United Press International.

Spencer Johnson's books are available worldwide in twenty-six languages.

To learn more, visit:
www.whomovedmycheese.com